E TYPE

JAGUAR

E TYPE

JAGUAR

ANDREW MORLAND

OSPREY
AUTOMOTIVE

Acknowledgement

The author and publisher would like to extend their sincere thanks to all of the owners of the cars photographed here; without their kind assistance the book would not have been possible. Thanks must also go to Vicarage Cars, Bridgenorth, Shropshire; Gran Turismo Jaguar, Eastlake, Ohio; Classic Car Specialists, Taunton, Somerset; Somerton Motor Co, Somerton, Somerset; Wildae Restorations, North Devon; Devon East Services, Burlescombe, Devon; the Jaguar Car Club; the Jaguar Drivers Club; and the Jaguar Enthusiasts Club.

Published in 1991 by Osprey Publishing Ltd
59 Grosvenor Street, London W1X 9DA

British Library Cataloguing in Publication Data

Morland, Andrew
 Jaguar E Type.
 1. Title
 629.2222

ISBN 185532184X

Editor Ian Penberthy
Page design Paul Kime
Printed in Hong Kong

Page 1
The E Type Jaguar is a classic shape from the 1960s. This one is a Series 1 4.2 litre fixed-head coupé

Page 2
A beautifully-restored, very early example of a 3.8 litre roadster

Right
Classic plate for a classic car

For a catalogue of all books published by Osprey Automotive please write to:

The Marketing Manager, Consumer Catalogue Department Osprey Publishing Ltd, 59 Grosvenor Street, London, W1X 9DA

Contents

Birth of a legend

It was in 1948, with Europe still recovering from the ravages of World War 2 and the British motor industry faced with having to export or die, that a long, sleek-looking sports car was introduced to the world by the newly-named Jaguar Cars Ltd. It was not, of course, the first Jaguar sports car, for the Jaguar name had been carried by a range of cars built before the war by SS Cars Ltd. However, the initials 'SS' had taken on a rather sinister connotation during the war years, and it was considered prudent to drop them in favour of 'Jaguar'.

The new sports car was the XK120, which had been conceived and built in a matter of weeks as a vehicle for Jaguar's new double-overhead-camshaft, in-line, six-cylinder engine. Of 3442 cc capacity, the new XK engine had a cast-iron block, an aluminium head and twin SU carburettors; it developed 160 bhp. Originally, the engine had been produced for a new high-performance saloon, but while both engine and chassis had been developed for this, the bodywork lagged far behind. Thus, the decision was taken to use a shortened version of the chassis and the engine beneath a beautifully-styled sports car body.

In this way, the XK120 came into being, not as part of a long-term strategy, but more as an expedient stop-gap measure. However, it was to have far-reaching consequences and became the forerunner of a range of sports cars that were to lead directly to the most famous of all the Jaguar sports cars – the E Type.

In those early post-war years, unitary body construction for cars was in its infancy, so the XK120 was based on a conventional, extremely rigid, separate chassis with a live axle at the rear suspended from a pair of semi-elliptic springs. At the front, however, was an independent suspension arrangement comprising double wishbones on each side with torsion-bar springing.

The body of the XK120 was intended to be built from aluminium in the traditional manner on an ash framework – indeed, the initial examples were built in this way – however, the demand for the car was so great, particularly from the United States, that this method of construction would have seriously restricted production. Thus, stronger pressed-steel panels were used, doing away with the need for the wooden framework.

The body itself was in two-seat open roadster style with a long, tapering bonnet and graceful, sweeping front wings, the line of which flowed back

In 1948, the newly-formed Jaguar Cars Ltd shocked everyone with the announcement of a long, sleek sports car powered by a new dohc in-line six-cylinder engine. It was the XK120, the first of a line of Jaguar sports cars that was to culminate in the E Type

through the doors to blend with the curved and tapered rear wings. The rear wheels were faired in, and there was a split windscreen with a polished frame.

The XK120 was an immediate success on both road and track. Its stylish good looks were matched by a comfortable ride and a top speed in excess of 100 mph – with a little aerodynamic help, the factory achieved 132 mph at Jabbeke in Belgium during 1949. In 1950, three XK120s were entered in the Le Mans 24-hour endurance race, and while they did not win, their performance encouraged the factory to purpose-build a competition version of the car specifically for that event, using the basic XK120 mechanical components. This was the XK120C, or C Type, which had the engine and front suspension of the road car in a lightweight tubular frame clad in a smooth aluminium bodyshell. Unlike the roadster, however, the rear axle was sprung by a transverse torsion bar.

Driven by Peter Whitehead and Peter Walker, a C Type won the 1951 Le Mans event, not only establishing the superiority of the XK120 engine, but also putting Jaguar well and truly on the map. An attempt to repeat this success in 1952 was terminated before the end of the race by cooling problems resulting from revised bodywork, but in 1953 the C Types returned with their normal bodywork and improved engines to win again, victory going to Duncan Hamilton and Tony Rolt.

Meanwhile the XK120 was winning a variety of other events, including road races and some tough rallies, such as the 1950 Alpine. The roadster had also been joined by a fixed-head coupé in 1951 and a drophead coupé in 1953. The former year had also seen the introduction of optional higher-lift cams that allowed the engine to develop an extra 20 bhp.

In 1954 the XK120 was replaced by the XK140, a more refined version of the earlier car with an engine that was rated at 190 bhp. In addition, it could be purchased with an optional C Type head that increased output to 210 bhp and gave a top speed that was just short of 130 mph. The XK120 had never been a 'blood and guts' sports car, the accent being more on comfortable, long-distance, high-speed touring, and the XK140 took this theme a step further, particularly with the availability of an automatic transmission from 1956, while those cars with a manual gearbox could be specified with an overdrive.

Comfort was not of prime concern on the race track, however, and for the 1954 Le Mans race, Jaguar pulled out the stops and arrived with a new racer – the D Type. The two-seat D Type had an aluminium monocoque body with a tubular subframe to carry the engine and front suspension. The body had sleek flowing lines – there was a small oval radiator air inlet, the headlights were faired over with clear plastic covers, there was a one-piece tilt front with a long, low hump in the bonnet to clear the dohc in-line six engine, a wrap-around clear plastic windscreen and a driver's headrest that was faired back into the bodywork. It was a beautiful, but purposeful-looking, car.

The stylish, flowing lines of the XK120
were ahead of their time. This
particular model was built in 1950
and is the oldest steel-bodied version
known to exist

The D Type came very close to winning that 1954 event and actually achieved victory a year later, in 1955, in the hands of Mike Hawthorn and Ivor Bueb. By 1956 the D Type's engine had grown to 3.8 litres and was equipped with a fuel-injection system. Although the works car was put out of the race when it crashed, one driven by the Ecurie Ecosse team took the chequered flag once more. Then, in 1957, the Jaguars took the first four places and a sixth in the world's most famous endurance race.

That year also saw the arrival of the XK150 as a replacement for the 140. This had new body styling, although it was clearly derived from the earlier XK cars, the most obvious change being the much higher line of the front wings where they flowed back through the doors to blend into the rear wings. Under the skin, much was the same, however, although the cars were equipped with disc brakes as standard, these having been developed on the C Type and D Type racers.

The engine could be had with an optional 'S' pack comprising triple SU carburettors and a straight-port head that increased power to 250 bhp, while two years later, in 1959, the capacity was increased to 3781 cc. In standard form, with twin carburettors, this developed 220 bhp, but with the optional head and triple carbs, 265 bhp was quoted.

Above
This clay model shows how the E Type was beginning to take shape as early as 1954. Note the long nose, faired-in headlights and tapered tail, all features that were to appear in 1961 when the E Type was unveiled

Right
The dohc, in-line, six-cylinder engine came from the XK150'S'. Of 3.8 litres, it was an impressive-looking powerplant capable of producing 265 bhp. All that aluminium means a lot of polishing, but the result is well worth it

However, while the 3.8-litre, dohc straight-six could be made to pump out plenty of power, as the 1960s dawned, the styling of the XK150 was beginning to look distinctly jaded, particularly when compared to the smooth flowing lines of the D Type racer. In fact, a few D Types were modified by Jaguar for road use, being sold under the title XK-SS. These incredibly fast machines were never intended to replace the XK150, however; Jaguar had been hard at work on that project since the mid 1950s.

In 1961, at the Geneva Motor Show, the covers were drawn back from a Jaguar sports car that was to become a legend. Its sleek, up-to-the-minute styling and technical specification were well ahead of its time and made the car the highlight of the show. The influence of the racing D Type could be clearly seen, not only in the body styling – which mirrored the D Type's flowing wings, faired-in headlights, and one-piece front with oval air inlet and central bulge – but also in the method of construction; the main portion of the body was of monocoque construction, while a tubular subframe carried the engine and front suspension. The last two items had come from the XK150 – the engine being to the 'S' specification – and, thus, could be traced back to the XK120. However, all similarities ended there, for the new car was the soon-to-be-famous E Type.

The E Type makes its début at the 1961 London Motor Show where, as it had done in Geneva, it stole the show. It was to become a legend among British sports cars

In the beginning . . .

When the covers came off the E Type in Geneva, it became the immediate star of the show. Here was a car that could keep pace with the more exotic names in the sports car world, had beautiful, sleek styling and offered tremendous value for money. Just as the XK120 had done before, it was to gain a vast following.

Two versions of the E type were available in this Series I guise, both two-seaters; there was an open roadster with a folding top, and a stylish fastback coupé with an opening rear hatch. Both were powered by the triple-carburettor, 'S'-specification, 3.8, dohc, in-line straight-six, which developed 265 bhp at 5500 rpm and 260 lb/ft of torque at 4000 rpm. This was sufficient to propel the car to a top speed of almost 150 mph and from rest to 60 mph in less than eight seconds. Moreover, it did so while returning in the region of 18 mpg.

Left
David Worrow's Series I 3.8 roadster is the 30th right-hand-drive roadster built, coming off the assembly line on 20 June 1961. It was featured on the Jaguar stand at that year's Motor Show in London

Above
All Series I E Types came with centre-lock wire wheels as standard. In those days, wires were de rigueur for any serious sports car. Note the Jaguar name on the hub cap

The D Type ancestry was quite unmistakeable, not just in the car's styling, but also in the mechanical specification. Although designed first and foremost as a road car, there was much in the E Type that was owed to racing practice – a clear example of racing improving the breed. Graham Hill was to prove that the car had a future on the track, too, by gaining its first racing victory in the year of its launch, driving a roadster to take the chequered flag in the GT Trophy race at Oulton Park.

Of particular interest was the E Type's rear suspension arrangement. A criticism of the earlier XK cars was that their rear suspension – a live axle suspended on semi-elliptic 'cart' springs – was somewhat antiquated for a high-performance car. Even the racing D Type's system, utilizing a transverse torsion bar, left a lot to be desired on many short circuits, although it was fine for long-distance endurance racing for which the car had been designed.

The E Type had an all-new independent rear suspension system, which was mounted in a steel cage that was bolted to the floorpan. Essentially a double-wishbone arrangement, it utilized the drive shafts as the upper 'wishbones'. Lower wishbones ran from the base of the differential to cast-aluminium hub carriers, while, on each side, a pair of coil-spring/damper units was attached between those lower wishbones and the top portion of

Above
Finished in Old English white, David Worrow's roadster was restored using all original parts to make it one of the most original E Types in the world. At the time these photographs were taken, in 1990, it had covered only 25,000 miles

Right
Another feature carried over from the D Type was the one-piece tilt front which provides plenty of access to the engine and other under-bonnet equipment. The cleanliness of David Worrow's example is a tribute to his efforts in restoring the car

the cage. Additional 'paddle-like' radius rods ran forwards from the lower wishbones to mountings beneath the floor. The brakes were discs, but mounted inboard on each side of the differential.

The front suspension was essentially the torsion-bar/double-wishbone arrangement from the XK series cars and D Type, while the steering was by rack and pinion.

Inside the car, the speedometer and tachometer were placed side by side and directly in front of the driver, behind the large-diameter wood-rim steering wheel, while auxiliary instruments and switches were grouped on an aluminium panel in the centre of the dashboard. The deep-section sills and central tunnel, which added considerable strength to the bodyshell, meant that the occupants sat low down inside it.

The 3.8 Series I E Type was a good car in terms of performance and appearance, but it could have been better. Originally, it was supplied with the XK series gearbox, which had no synchromesh on first gear and a wide

Left
Every aspect of the roadster has been lovingly restored. Note the position of the dynamo close to the forward exhaust manifold — the heat from the latter did nothing to prolong the former's life

Above
The triple SU carburettors are connected to a cylindrical air filter, behind the offside front wheel, by a large triangular plenum chamber. Early examples of the car, like this one, had a special key with which the bonnet catches were released; later, a remote control was provided

gap between that gear and second, while the seats left much to be desired in terms of support on long runs. In 1964, however, both drawbacks were taken care of with a new all-synchro box and wider, more supportive seats. That was not the limit of alterations, however, for that year also saw the introduction of the 4.2 litre version of the dohc straight-six. Of 4235 cc capacity, the engine was still rated at 265 bhp, but at 5400 rpm and with greater torque – 283 lb/ft at 4000 rpm. At the same time, the dynamo was replaced by an alternator and the cooling system was improved, along with a range of other minor details. However, the car remained designated Series I.

In 1966 a new model was announced to run alongside the original roadster and coupé. This was the 2+2, which was available as a fixed-head coupé only and had a 9 in. longer wheelbase to allow the installation of two small, folding rear seats. These were really only suitable for children; in the standard coupé, the space behind the seats acted simply as a load platform for carrying luggage.

To provide the necessary headroom for rear-seat passengers, the roofline, side windows and windscreen were increased in height, the windscreen

Above
The Series I dashboard had a central aluminium panel to carry the auxiliary instruments and switchgear. The ignition was controlled by a key, but there was a separate starter button on the panel

Right
The beautiful interior of David Worrow's car. At one time, it was used as a demonstrator by Henleys in Central London. Deep sills and transmission tunnel added strength to the monocoque body

itself having a more upright appearance. Although making the car more practical for the family man, the changes tended to spoil the proportions of the sleek coupé body.

All three models continued in production virtually unchanged for another year. Then, in late 1967, the transparent headlight covers were dispensed with and a wide-ratio gearbox, previously fitted to the 2+2 and coupé models, was fitted to the roadster. Various other minor changes were also made at this time, and these cars are often termed Series I½. They covered the transition period up to the launch of the next version of the E Type, which was announced in October 1968 as the Series II.

Above
The E Type's shape stunned the motoring public when it appeared, and even today, it is a head-turner. Note the deep return under the rear of the body and the upswept exhaust system

Right
Many early E Types were built with triple windscreen wipers. Those louvres in the bonnet were as much functional as aesthetic, since the car could suffer from overheating

Another very early 3.8 roadster is this
example belonging to Bill Cooke, who
operates his own restoration business
– Wildae Restorations Ltd. The E Type
is a good example of his work,
although it is not quite totally original
– the headlight buckets should be
finished in silver, not red

Left
The engine in Bill Cooke's roadster is a testimony to his restoration skills. The tilt front makes access so easy, which cannot be said of so many modern sports cars

Right
The bucket seats of the early 3.8 E Types came in for criticism for the lack of support provided on long journeys. This was not to be rectified until the advent of the 4.2 litre version. Occupants had to step over the sill and down into the car

Above
Only 756 right-hand-drive 3.8 litre roadsters were built – this one is number 28. The woodrim steering wheel came from a later car

Right
E Types look all the more dashing when finished in bright red. The folding top can be stowed beneath a neat tonneau when not in use

Above
Shaun Baker owns this 3.8 litre Series I fixed-head coupé. The sleek tapering roof line made the coupé particularly attractive, while the opening rear hatch made it a very practical GT car

Right
The engine room of the E Type is an impressive sight with those polished aluminium cam covers and the row of SU carburettors

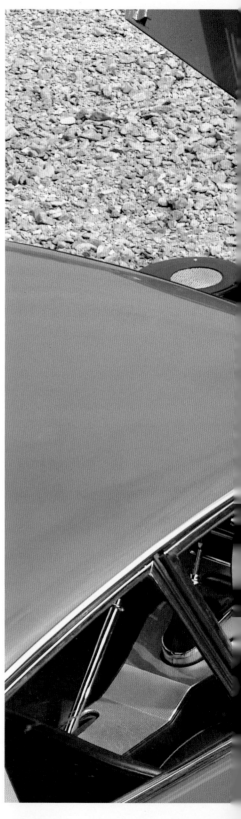

Above
Although accentuated by this low-level photograph, the E Type had quite a generous ground clearance. The depth of the sills is evident

Right
Shaun Baker's coupé was originally built as a left-hand-drive model and sent to Belgium. However, on its return to this country, it was converted to right-hand-drive by Jaguar. Many owners preferred the early toggle switches on the instrument panel since there was no doubting from their position whether they were 'on' or 'off'

Above
*The clear covers over the headlights
did much to make the front end look
sleek, but the side lights always looked
as though they had been added as
afterthoughts. The oval radiator air
intake was to remain without a grille
until the advent of the Series III*

Left
*In 1965 the E Type received the 4.2
litre version of the dohc straight-six
and with it a new gearbox and better
seats. However, from the outside there
is nothing to suggest that there is
anything different about the car, as
can be seen from this beautiful
example owned by Peter Lawton*

Above
Like the front side lights, the rear lights also looked as though they had been stuck on at the last moment, spoiling the otherwise stylish lines of the car

Left
The big cylindrical air filter housing occupied a considerable amount of space behind the front wheel

Above

Of course, cars are built for driving, and driving an E Type can be a lot of fun, as L. Rodwell can testify. His opalescent silver-blue 4.2 fixed-head coupé was first registered in 1964, when it was sold to a Mr Gill by the Tourist Trophy Garage in Farnham, Surrey, for the princely sum of £2039 16s 8d – and that included £15 road tax. Those were the days!

Left

First registered in May 1965, Peter Lawton's Series I 4.2 litre coupé is a prime example of the GT car. The dark green opalescent metallic paint looks so deep that you could almost fall into it

Although the 4.2 litre engine developed 265 bhp like the earlier 3.8 version, it produced more torque (283 lb/ft as opposed to 260 lb/ft, both at 4000 rpm) to make it more flexible

Left
The long nose with its central power bulge and faired-in headlights owed so much to the D Type. The stick-on number plate was a necessity, but it was far from legal, although most members of the constabulary turned a blind eye

Above
The large-diameter woodrim steering wheel was in the true sports car tradition – and necessary to gain enough leverage to turn the 15 in. diameter crossply tyres. Note the lack of aluminium finish on the central panel of this later car

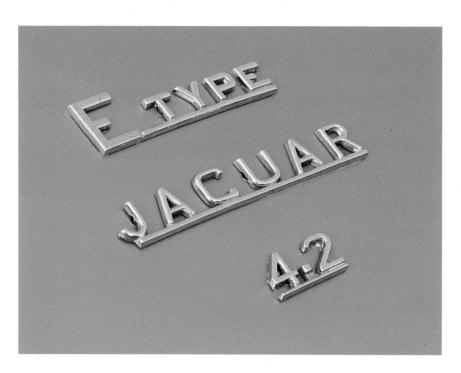

Above
The legend on the rear hatch is simple and to the point, unlike the cluttered mass of different type faces found on many of today's cars

Right
The flat load platform behind the seats of the fixed-head coupé provided plenty of room for luggage when touring, although that luggage was exposed for all and sundry to see. The spare wheel was kept below the floor, which could make dealing with a puncture a real pain when carrying a full load

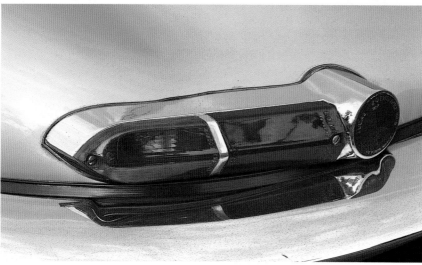

Top
A neat, spring-loaded door in the nearside rear wing conceals the fuel tank filler cap. The tank itself has a capacity of 14 imperial gallons

Above
Functional, rather than stylish, the rear lights on the Series I cars were mounted above the wrap-around rear bumpers

Right
Despite the long nose, the fixed-head coupé has a balanced line. Even today, it turns heads

Top
*The classic Jaguar emblem that
seemed to float on its bar in the centre
of the oval radiator air inlet*

Left
*In 1966 a third model of E Type was
launched – the 2+2. This had a longer
wheelbase (8 ft 9 in. instead of 8 ft) to
allow the installation of two small rear
seats. It was available as a fixed-head
coupé only*

Above
*Set deep in their recesses, behind clear
covers, the headlights were not known
for their candle power – but they
certainly looked the part*

Above
*Attention to detail is essential to the
success of any restoration*

Left
*The exhaust manifolds comprised two
banks of three; note the shielding for
the alternator. Keeping an engine as
spotless as this means many hours of
work – or never using the car at all!*

Above
*Jim Longley's Series I 4.2 litre 2 + 2 is
finished in opalescent silver blue. The
four seat model had a longer door and
deeper side windows, the latter due to
a higher roof line necessary to give
enough headroom in the rear*

Right
*The rear seats of the 2 + 2 are really
only suitable for children, the upper
portion of the seat back folding
forwards to increase the size of the
load platform when needed*

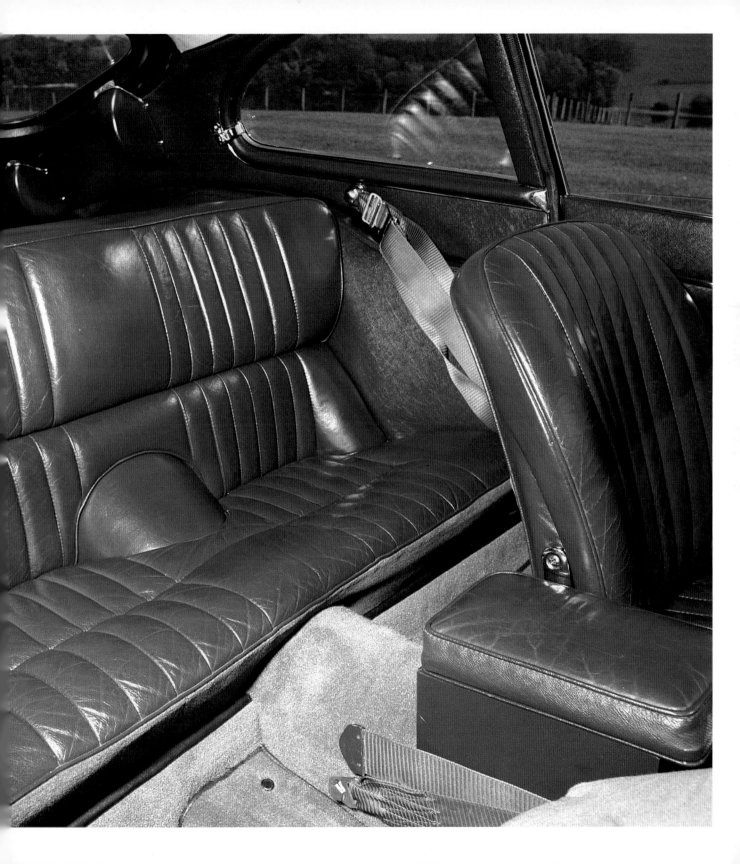

Above
The hinged rear hatch was a great asset for loading luggage

Right
Jim Longley restored his 2 + 2 himself – according to the chassis number, it is the 161st example of the model built in right-hand-drive form

Above
*Long and lean, the Series I roadster is
a beautiful car*

Left
*In late 1967, various changes were
made to the E Type in preparation for
the launch of the Series II. One of the
changes was the removal of the
headlight covers, the lights being
pulled forwards. These interim models
were known as Series I½, of which this
2+2 is an example*

Above
*Sets of louvres on each side of the
central power bulge provide an accent
to the bonnet top and allow some of
the heat generated by the in-line six to
escape*

Right
A delight from every angle

CAUTION
THE ELECTRICAL SYSTEM POLARITY
ON THIS VEHICLE IS
NEGATIVE EARTH
CORRECT BATTERY POLARITY
MUST BE

Left
*Everything is easily to hand beneath
the E Type's bonnet, although the
proximity of the exhaust manifolds to
various electrical items could cause
problems*

Above
*When John Stott is at work for the
Royal Navy, he spends his time
beneath the ocean in a submarine, so
no wonder he looks forward to a breath
of fresh air in this bright red Series I
roadster*

Top
This shot shows just what a long, sleek car the E Type is. The styling was the work of Malcolm Sayer

Above
The E Type provides an elegant and powerful manner of open-top transportation

Left
The 1965 4.2 roadster is seen here on Dartmoor with its happy submariner owner enjoying the summer sunshine

Above
*The roomy cockpit of the Series I
roadster is neatly laid out. John Stott's
example is in excellent condition*

Right
*There is no mistaking the D Type
ancestry from this angle. However,
the E Type was definitely a road car
and while it enjoyed competition
success, it was not to score
significantly in long-distance
endurance races*

For safety's sake

The increasing emphasis on vehicle safety in the late 1960s caused a major revision of the E Type, leading to the Series II that arrived in October 1968. Externally, there were some significant changes in its appearance, which made it look a little less sleek than its forebears and had a noticeable negative effect on the car's performance.

At the front, the oval radiator air intake had been enlarged to give something like a 68 per cent increase in cross-section, while the headlights – no longer behind their clear covers – were pulled forwards so that they protruded from the oval recesses in the front.

The side, indicator and rear lights, which had always looked as though they had been stuck on to the car as afterthoughts were increased in size and moved below the bumpers at front and rear. While this tended to help the visual appearance of the car, they still looked like afterthoughts and were to remain so for the rest of the car's life.

One other significant exterior change was that the rake of the windscreen on the roadster and standard coupé was steepened to match that of the 2+2. All these exterior changes were to increase the drag produced by the body shape, leading to a decrease in top speed of some 10 mph.

Mechanically, little was changed on the Series II cars, although the increased cooling air aperture was matched by a new vertical-flow radiator and expansion tank, twin thermostatically-controlled electric cooling fans and a revised water pump. The front brakes were also improved with new three-piston calipers, and the hubs and spokes of the wire wheels were strengthened.

Inside, several changes were made to improve the safety of the occupants in the event of an accident. Door handles were recessed and the row of toggle switches on the dashboard was replaced by a line of rocker types. The layout of the instruments remained essentially the same, but the clock, which previously had been set into the face of the tachometer, was moved to the centre of the auxiliary instrument/switch panel.

The Series II was to continue in production until 1971 with only minor changes, among them redesigned camshafts for quieter running, an improved ignition system, 'earless' hubcaps (to avoid carving up pedestrians' legs) and optional steel disc wheels.

The next E Type to appear, the Series III, although looking very similar, was significantly different, particularly under the bonnet.

The Series II E Type arrived in 1968, displaying a few external changes, although mechanically, it was essentially the same as the earlier cars. This beautiful roadster was provided by Somerton Motor Company and is a prime example of their restoration work

Above
Side-on, there is little difference between the Series II and the Series I. Most obvious changes are to the side light positions, front and rear, which are now beneath the bumpers. This model also lacks the 'ears' on the hubcaps

Right
The interior of the Series II was also changed – notice the lid on the glove box and the row of rocker switches in place of the earlier toggle types. The clock was also moved from the tachometer to the centre of the auxiliary instrument panel

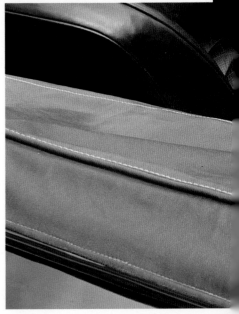

Above
*The black finish on the Somerton
Motors Series II is unusual and gives a
very sophisticated look to the car,
which is neatly set off by the chrome of
the bumpers and wire wheels*

Right
*This angle clearly shows the revised
headlight treatment; the covers were
removed and the light units pulled
forwards, which rather spoiled the
sleek appearance of the car*

The tail came in for a revision as well, the number plate recess being altered and the rear quarter bumpers being joined by a central piece. Note the larger, repositioned rear lights

Above
The higher roof line, wider door and deeper side windows of the 2 + 2 can be clearly seen in this photograph. These features tended to detract a little from the sleek appearance of the standard fixed-head coupé

Right
This 1969 2 + 2 Series II began life as a left-hand-drive model and previously was owned by a US serviceman serving in Norfolk. Its present owner, M. Cripps, bought the car from him and converted it to right-hand-drive

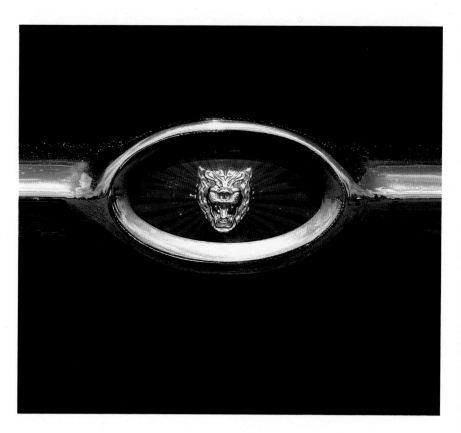

Above
The Series II had an oval emblem in the centre of its radiator air inlet bar

Right
The overall layout beneath the bonnet of the Series II is essentially the same as that of the Series I. However, note the different cam covers

Above
*Finished in Signal red, M. Cripps'
2+2 is a prime example of the breed.
Not only did the present owner convert
it to right-hand-drive, but he restored
it as well*

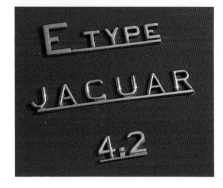

Right
Just in case you were in any doubt

Left
*One thing for sure is that the E Type
was never styled to have a front
number plate. The normal stick-on
type is an unsightly blemish on its nose
(and illegal to boot), while there is
nowhere suitable to hang a rigid
separate plate, as can be seen here*

Above
Sadly, the stylists never got the rear-end treatment quite right. Above the bumper it is fine, but below it is a mish-mash of bits and pieces, hung here and there. This lack of thought spoiled an otherwise fine design

Right
The fixed-head coupé had a beautiful line to the rear, as can be seen from these Series II models

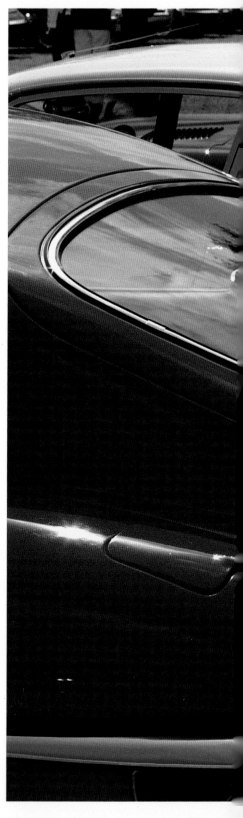

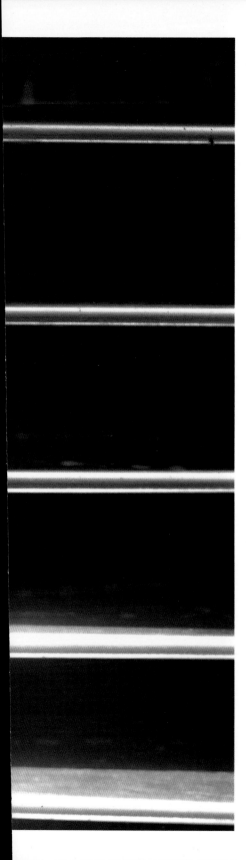

V12 and beyond

In 1971 the E Type received the most substantial and last major change of its life with the introduction of the Series III. Like the XK120 so many years before, the Series III was to allow Jaguar to introduce a new engine and gain valuable experience with it on a limited production basis before slotting it into its intended home – the XJ saloon. It was, of course, the all-aluminium 5.3 litre V12.

With an actual capacity of 5343 cc, the V12 had a single overhead camshaft for each bank of six cylinders and was fed fuel by four Stromberg carburettors. The heads were of a flat design, the combustion chambers being incorporated in the piston crowns. Capable of developing 314 bhp at 6200 rpm and 349 lb/ft of torque at 3600 rpm, it was a very flexible and smooth engine that overcame the drop in performance experienced by the six-cylinder models as a result of increasingly strict exhaust emission regulations, albeit with an increase in fuel consumption to 15 mpg.

Two versions of the Series III E Type were available, a two-seat roadster and a 2+2 coupé, both based on the long-wheelbase floorpan previously used only by the latter. However, external modifications to the bodywork led to it gaining a slightly portly appearance. The overall shape was maintained, but the wheel arches were flared to cover wider tyres, a slatted grille was added to the radiator air inlet in the one-piece tilt front, and further cooling air was admitted by a 'chin' scoop.

In addition to the new engine, the braking system was uprated with ventilated front discs, while power steering became standard equipment. Both were essential because of the increased weight of the car. As standard, the Series III came with steel disc wheels, while a set of chromed wires was available as an option.

All in all, the V12 Series III was a much heavier car than its six-cylinder predecessors, and the extra weight, coupled with the long wheelbase, did nothing to improve the car's handling or braking performance. While putting the engine in the E Type allowed Jaguar to gain experience with it prior to its use in far greater numbers in the XJ saloon, in truth, it outpaced chassis development of the sports car, turning it into a high-speed tourer.

The E Type story does not end there, however, for by the time that production came to a halt, the car had become a legend with an enthusiastic following. That following is no less enthusiastic today.

In an era when the computerization of car design has led to a lack of individuality between the many various marques, and the high-revving, turbocharged four-cylinder engine has become the norm, the sleek shape of the E Type and its lazy, but powerful, in-line six or V12 is enough to set the pulse of any true sports car fan racing. Those that survive are assured a secure future and will continue to be in demand, taking their rightful place among the great classic cars.

Previous page
The arrival of the Series III in 1971 brought a new radiator air inlet treatment – for the first time, the E Type had a grille, which had a gold-finished badge in the centre

Right
Not all Series III cars were equipped with the V12 engine. This prototype roadster has the 4.2 litre in-line six of the earlier cars. The flared wheel arches make the car look much wider than before

Far right
The dohc in-line six in the Series III prototype. Note the Stromberg carburettors, the different carburettor air inlet arrangement and the new position for the battery

Above
Syd Taylor's Old English white Series III roadster was first registered in March 1974. At the time these photographs were taken in 1990, it had only 7100 miles on the clock

Left
The Series III was equipped with this type of pressed steel disc wheel as standard, rather than the wires of the earlier cars. They detracted somewhat from the sporting appearance of the car, but were a lot more practical and stronger

The factory hardtop made the roadster a really practical car for year-round driving

Above
Owned by Bert Knight, this Series III is equipped with the optional wire wheels. Although there was not much difference in the width of the Series III cars, they looked a lot 'tubbier'

Left
To provide the additional airflow needed to cool the big V12 engine, the Series III E Type was fitted with a chin scoop beneath the main oval air inlet. The 'leaping Jaguar' bonnet mascot is definitely not original equipment

Overleaf
Originally, it had been intended for the V12 to be fuel injected from the outset, but the development work came to a halt when Jaguar's partner in the project pulled out. Thus, the engine was equipped with four Stromberg carburettors

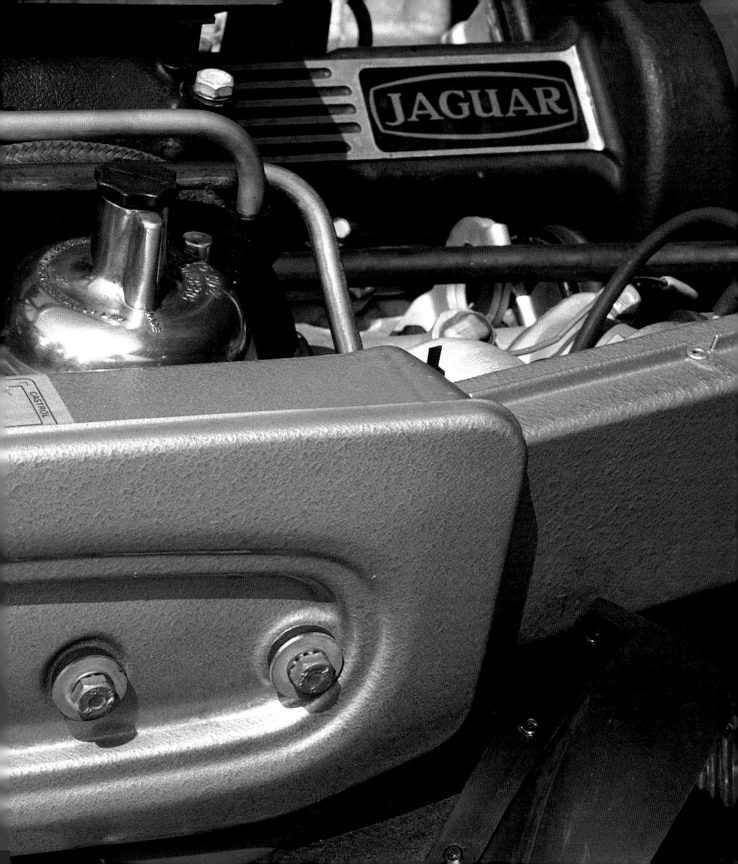

Above
All Series III cars were based on the 8ft 9in. wheelbase floorpan of the earlier 2+2, although the roadsters only had two seats. This was perhaps a trifle too long for the open cars

Right
Dashboard of the Series III belonging to Bert Knight. It is very similar in layout to the Series II model

Above
Rear-end treatment is also similar to the Series II, but note the four exhaust outlets and the wider tyres

Right
Only two models of Series III were made: the two-seat roadster and the 2+2 fixed-head coupé. This 1973 example of the latter belongs to Tom Evans and is equipped with a sliding sunroof

Above
*The high roofline and deeper side
windows of the 2+2 coupé bodyshell
are quite obvious in this picture*

Right
*The greater width of the V12 engine
required a wider subframe to support
it. Note the air filtration arrangement
for the carburettors*

Above
*Finished in Azure blue, Tom Evans'
Series III is an immaculate example
of the breed*

Right
*It is remarkable how little the
dashboard layout of the E Type
changed over the years. The steering
wheel was no longer of the woodrim
variety, but still surprisingly large
considering that power steering was
standard equipment*

Above
The sunshine roof in Tom Evans' car allows him to enjoy open-air motoring when the weather is kind, yet have the benefits of the 2 + 2 fixed-head coupé when it is not

Right
The rear hatch of the 2 + 2 coupé told the story – if you were in any doubt

The last 50 E Types built were sold as Commemorative models. This one, belonging to David Dacombe, was number 28 in that batch of 50. It left the factory in late 1974 and had only covered 27,700 miles by the time it was photographed in 1990

Above
Finished in black with the optional wire wheels, David Dacombe's Series III roadster is certainly an impressive-looking car

Right
In all that time, nothing was done about the headlamps, which looked like an interim measure, half-way between the original neatly-covered versions and something that blended in with the styling. The flared wheelarch can be clearly seen

Above
Some of the litheness had definitely disappeared with the Series III

Right
The Vicarage company has made a name for itself by specializing in restoring Jaguars of all types and in rebuilding them to a modern specification, using many more modern mechanical components. This example of a Series III V12 roadster has been rebuilt by them

Above
The Series III roadster is a long car, as can be seen from this photograph of the Vicarage version. The company offers a wide range of options, including a Getrag five-speed manual gearbox in place of the standard automatic or four-speed

Right
Neatly restored dashboard in the Vicarage Series III V12. As an option, the company can provide a wood finish for the three panels

Previous page
The V12 engine filled the engine compartment of the E Type, but the flip-forward front end made servicing much easier than on the saloons which used the engine. The Vicarage version can be supplied with a GT package and air-conditioning equipment

Above
The tail treatment of the Series III still left a lot to be desired – revised light units incorporating reversing lights would have allowed the number plate to be fitted snugly beneath the central portion of the bumper rather than hanging down in the wind

Right
Beautifully trimmed in leather, the interior of the Vicarage E Type roadster includes an optional full rear seat. Head restraints are standard on the front seats

Above

Engines are rebuilt with precision and are probably in better condition than when they left the factory

Left

The craftsmen at Vicarage do a thorough job of restoration – every car is rebuilt from the ground up. Here a Series I fixed-head coupé bodyshell is undergoing the treatment

Above
*Bodyshells are completely stripped,
repaired as necessary and then
repainted. This one is a Series I
roadster*

Left
*A dohc in-line six is run-in on the
engine test rig*

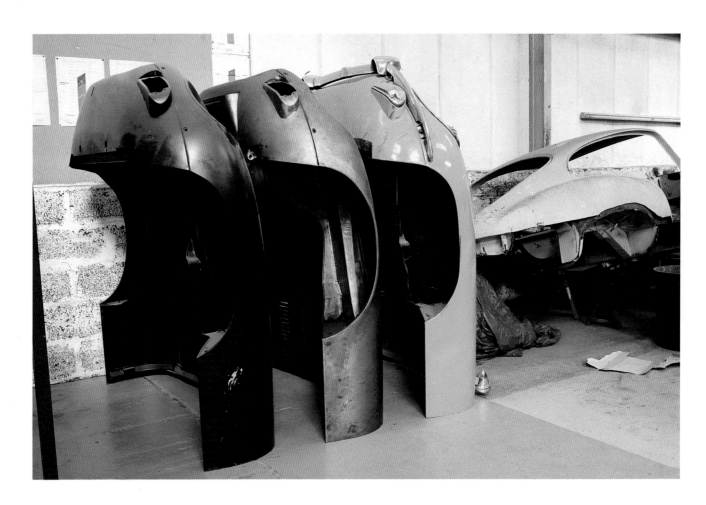

*New and old front ends stand waiting
to be fitted*

All the paintwork is protected to prevent damage during the reassembly of the car

Above
Not all E Types are restored to their
original condition, which might upset
some enthusiasts. Nick Packard
decided that his Series I roadster could
do with a few modifications, and after
2000 hours of work, the result is what
you see here

Left
The front end of a Series I undergoes
repair and restoration in the Vicarage
workshop

Above
*Nick Packard's E Type certainly looks
tough as a result of several body
modifications. If they don't make it
stand out from the crowd, the flawless,
bright red paint does*

Left
*The engine in Nick Packard's roadster
is a high-compression 4.2 litre in-line
six equipped with triple Weber
carburettors, big valves and special
camshafts; it produces 230 bhp at the
rear wheels*

Above
*Impressive-looking Weber
carburettors have obviously seen
plenty of use*

Right
*The rear wings were widened to cover
the Goodrich Comp T/A tyres and have
scoops formed in their leading edges*

The lack of bumpers seems to emphasize the length of the E Type nose on Nick Packard's Series I. What the aficionados think of it, goodness only knows